A Special Gift for

with love,

date

To my mother

When people tell me I remind them of you,
I tell them that's the best compliment
they could ever pay me.
Your spirit of warmth, conviction,
integrity, and unconditional love
has done much to fashion me into the
woman and mother I am today.

I love you.

Stories, sayings, and scriptures to Encourage and Inspire

hugs™
for Mom
Book 2

PHILIS BOULTINGHOUSE
Personalized Scriptures by
LEANN WEISS

★ HOWARD
PUBLISHING CO.

Our purpose at Howard Publishing is to:

- *Increase faith* in the hearts of growing Christians
- *Inspire holiness* in the lives of believers
- *Instill hope* in the hearts of struggling people everywhere

Because He's coming again!

Hugs for Mom, Book 2 © 2004 by Philis Boultinghouse
All rights reserved. Printed in the United States of America
Published by Howard Publishing Co., Inc.
3117 North 7th Street, West Monroe, LA 71291-2227
www.howardpublishing.com

04 05 06 07 08 09 10 11 12 13   10 9 8 7 6 5 4 3 2

Paraphrased scriptures © 2004 LeAnn Weiss, 3006 Brandywine Dr.
Orlando, FL 32806; 407-898-4410

Edited by Between the Lines
Interior design by Stephanie D. Walker
Photography by LinDee Loveland

Library of Congress Cataloging-in-Publication Data
Boultinghouse, Philis, 1951–
   Hugs for mom : stories, sayings, and scriptures to encourage and inspire / Philis
Boultinghouse ; personalized scriptures by LeAnn Weiss.
      p. cm.
   "Book 2."
   Includes index.
   ISBN: 1-58229-371-6
      1. Mothers—Religious life. 2. Christian women—Religious life. 3. Motherhood—
Religious aspects—Christianity. I. Weiss, LeAnn. II. Title.

BV4529.18.B68 2004
242'.6431—dc22

                                                            2004047357

Contents

1

a mother's home

home

$\mathcal{W}$hen you wait upon Me, I'll re-energize you and help you to thrive. Build your home with My wisdom and establish it through understanding. Use knowledge to fill its rooms with treasures rare and beautiful. When you hope in Me, you'll never be disappointed.

Renewing you,
Your Creator

—from Isaiah 40:31; Proverbs 24:3–4; Isaiah 49:23

3

Mothers are the builders of home.

You don't need a special degree or elaborate training. Previous experience is not required. A home is not measured by the number of rooms or the height of the ceilings. It's not defined by how many people live in the house or what kind of neighborhood it's in. It doesn't matter if you're surrounded by extended family or in a new place on your own. In fact, a home is not a physical thing at all.

A home is warmth and hope and support. It's laughter and joy and peace. It's sadness shared and disappointments understood. It's the freedom to grieve and the encouragement to dream. A home is people and relationships. Mostly, a home is love.

But a home does not build itself. It takes effort and determination. It requires purpose and vision. Sometimes it means behaving contrary to the way you feel: getting up when you feel like staying down, moving forward when you're stuck in the past. While building a home takes great effort, it's not beyond your reach. You have within you all that's required to make a true home for those you love.

You have hands that caress and arms that embrace. You have a voice that encourages and lips full of kisses. You have feet that run to help and ears that listen. You have a heart that cares and a love that shares. You are a mother, the builder of your home.

*P*leasant memories
can give us an immediate
cheer-producing mind switch.

Marilyn Meberg

Ruth was disconnected
from all that had
made her feel a part—
a part of something
bigger than herself
and her little family.

Threads of Love

Ruth's eyes glazed over as she stared out the window above her kitchen sink. No matter how hard she tried, she just couldn't call this little rent-house home. It was a house. Nothing more. She had no roots here, no connections. Ruth had left all her connections back home in southern California where she'd grown up—where all her family still lived.

At first Ruth had been thrilled with Kurt's job offer. A job with a national insurance firm would provide the security they desperately needed for their little family of three. But as the time approached for leaving all that was familiar, Ruth's confidence in their decision dwindled. She'd never lived away from her family before. Who would baby-sit when she and Kurt needed an evening out? Who would make birthdays special? Who would help her teach Crystal all she needed to know? The answer was simple: there would be no one. She was alone.

Of course she had Kurt. And Crystal. She loved being a wife and mom—she really did. But she had grown up part of a big, busy family, and now her family was so small. She was disconnected from all that had made her feel a part—a part of something bigger than herself and her little family.

Ruth finished the dishes, then plopped down on the couch and waited for the bus to bring Crystal home from school. She leaned her head back and closed her eyes. In her mind she was seven years old again and sitting on a footstool at her grandmother's feet. Mama Lou pulled a spool of thread from the top shelf of her sewing chest. The chest stood about twenty-seven inches tall and was made of two beautiful woods—one light and one dark—alternately inlaid for a striped effect. Two drawers held scissors, thimbles, and miscellaneous sewing accessories. A hidden shelf with built-in spool dowels was revealed when the top was opened. Ruth loved the old chest, partly because it was beautiful and partly because the grandfather she barely remembered had made it. But mostly because it reminded her of family.

Mama Lou was threading a needle with a blue thread that perfectly matched the button that had fallen from Ruth's jacket. "Once you have the needle threaded, you tie a knot in the end of the thread, like this." Mama Lou deftly looped the thread around her index finger, twisted it between her thumb and forefinger, and then slid the twisted thread between her thumbnail and finger until it caught in a knot. She held it up for Ruth to see.

"Now you try it," Mama Lou said, handing Ruth a piece of thread. Ruth twisted the thread as she had seen Mama Lou do and pulled it between her fingers, but no knot appeared.

"I can't do it," she pouted. "I never can do anything right!"

"Lands sakes alive!" Mama Lou retorted. "Of course you can! You do all sorts of things right. Why, just this morning I saw you helping your mother make banana pancakes, and they were delicious. Here, watch me one more time."

After watching Mama Lou a second time, Ruth picked up her thread. Sticking her tongue out the corner of her mouth and furrowing her brow in deep concentration, she looped and twisted and slid the thread once again. "I did it, Mama Lou," she exulted. "I did it! I made a knot."

"Of course you did." Mama Lou resumed her sewing matter-of-factly. "You can do most anything you set your mind to."

Ruth had beamed with confidence that day long ago. She had felt she could indeed do anything. But now, twenty years later, Mama Lou was long gone, and Ruth felt anything but confident. *How am I going to handle Crystal's first crush? I had my mother, my grandmother, and several aunts to help me recover from my first broken heart. And how will Crystal feel with just her dad and me cheering her on at school plays and sporting events? My cheering section was three full rows. I don't like living away from family!*

Just then Ruth heard the door open, and Crystal burst into the room crying. Ruth was kneeling in front of her daughter in seconds. "What is it, honey? What happened?"

Huge tears rolled down Crystal's red cheeks. "Laura and Misty wouldn't let me play with them," she said, her little chest heaving with emotion. "They said I wasn't part of their group! They said they were best friends in kindergarten and first grade, and I just moved here, so they won't let me be their friend."

"Oh, I'm so sorry, honey. I'm sure there are plenty of other girls you can be friends with," Ruth said, feeling not nearly as confident as she tried to sound.

"Why did we have to move away from Grandma and Grandpa? I liked my old school and my old friends! Can we move back, Mommy, can we please?"

I'd do it in a heartbeat if it were up to me, Ruth thought to herself, but aloud she said, "We've only been here a few weeks. It takes time to get used to new people and places. You'll make some friends, honey, you just wait and see."

"Do you really think so, Mommy?" Crystal's crying had slowed, and she looked at Ruth with eyes full of hope and trust.

"I know so." Ruth gathered her daughter in her arms and gave her an assuring hug. *I've only been away from my family three weeks, and I'm telling my daughter a bold-faced lie. I need my mother!* Ruth fought back her own tears as she comforted her trusting daughter. "It's going to be OK . . . it's going to be just fine." But Ruth didn't believe a word of it.

The sharp ring of the doorbell made both Ruth and

Crystal jump. "Who could that be?" Ruth said as she straightened her hair and gathered her composure. She opened the door to a uniformed delivery person.

"Package for you, ma'am," the young man said. "Please sign here."

Ruth signed for the package and pulled it inside. Tears sprang to her eyes as soon as the door closed. The return address was Cool Valley Road, the California street where her mom and dad lived. It must be another care package from her mother. Last week she had sent a big box with Ruth's two favorite kinds of candy—plain and peanut M&M's—and wheat bread and granola from her favorite health-food store. "I wonder what Grandma has sent us this time?" Ruth said to Crystal. "Why don't you help me open this big box."

Pulling off the many layers of wrapping tape, Ruth finally got the box open. Now she had to dig through several layers of packing paper and peanuts. "Grandma really knows how to keep stuff safe."

Ruth caught her breath, and her tears now flowed unrestrained. She couldn't believe what she saw.

Threads of Love

"Why are you crying, Mommy?" Crystal asked. "Don't you like our present?"

"I love it. Sometimes mommies cry when they're happy. Here, you hold the box while I pull out Grandma's surprise."

Slowly, carefully, Ruth pulled out the family heirloom that meant more to her than any other piece of furniture in her mother's house. "It's Mama Lou's sewing chest, Crystal. Grandma has sent me Mama Lou's sewing chest!"

"It's striped—like a zebra." Crystal mused, running her fingers over the inlaid wood. "What's a sewing chest?"

"It's a special place to keep needles and thread and buttons and scissors. See?" Ruth opened one side of the hinged top to reveal several old wooden spools of thread mounted on tiny dowels. "Crystal, look. The spools have writing on them. This one says 'For gold slacks.' Here's another one that says 'For JoAnn's jacket.' *JoAnn* is your Grandma's name."

Ruth picked up a spool of blue thread. "For Ruth's blue—" Fresh tears filled her eyes. "This is the thread Mama Lou used to sew a button on my jacket when I was a little girl— just about your age." Ruth gently pulled open one of the drawers. Her grandfather's craftsmanship was evident in the chest's tiniest details. Even after all these years, the drawer slid out smoothly, without a hitch. Inside the drawer was a note in her mother's handwriting:

I thought you could use a little reminder of home to help you feel connected with all of us here who love you so much. I'm so proud of you for stepping out to make a home for yourself in a new place. May these threads from the past be a link to your future.

> *Love,*
> *Mom*

"Crystal, bring me your red shirt with the missing button. I'll fix it for you like Mama Lou used to fix my clothes for me."

Crystal quickly retrieved it and then sat on the ottoman by Ruth's chair. She watched intently as Ruth rummaged through the thread looking for just the right color.

"Once you have the needle threaded, you tie a knot in the end of the thread, like this." Ruth deftly looped the thread around her index finger, twisted it between her thumb and forefinger, and then slid the twisted thread between her thumbnail and finger until it caught in a knot. She held it up for Crystal to see.

"Now, you try it." Ruth smiled as Crystal made her first attempt at threading a needle.

For the first time in a long time, Ruth felt peaceful and whole. Distance could not break the connection with her family. They were all irrevocably linked—Mama Lou, her own mother, herself, and now Crystal—held together by threads of love that spanned both space and time.

2

a mother's strength

strength

$\mathcal{I}$n the midst of the challenges of motherhood, take time to be still and know that I am God. Remember that I'm in control. *Nothing* is too difficult with Me leading your team. You can fulfill all your responsibilities because I strengthen you today and always!

Encouraging you,
Your All-Powerful God

—from Psalm 46:10; Luke 1:37; Philippians 4:13

Life is fragile. That's why God made mothers strong.

Oh, moms may not *seem* all that strong. Mothers are soft and flexible. They're gentle and tender. Not the kind of words you'd use to describe strength. And moms cry. A mom will cry when her five-year-old son crosses the stage at kindergarten graduation. She'll cry when her little girl picks a handful of weeds from the backyard and presents them with a flourish as a gift of her love.

But don't let those tears fool you. They disguise a strength that is beyond the physical, an endurance that defies reason. When a child is mistreated—whether by an adult or another child—a mother will defend and protect. When a child feels defeated or discouraged, a mom will rehearse all the achievements—past, present, and future—of that vulnerable child. And when a child fights against the mother who loves her, that mother's heart and soul will go into overdrive to figure out how to reach that wayward heart and bring it home again.

A mother's understanding of the past instills her with wisdom to make better choices in the future. A mother's handle on the present empowers her to guard her words in stressful situations and smile when she's too tired to think. A mother's vision for the future allows her to see what her children can become and gives her the strength to hold on until her dreams for tomorrow become the reality of today.

*I*t takes a long, long time
for the deep hurts to be resolved—
sometimes it feels like forever.
Hang in there! As someone once said,
genuine healing is not
a microwave process.
It's more like a Crockpot experience.

Barbara Johnson

Joan watched Liana

stomp off, the wall

between them

growing more real

with every step.

The Blessing of Silence

"I feel like I'm losing her, Sam. There's a wall growing up between us. We don't talk anymore. She hardly even looks at me."

"You're overreacting, Joan. She's just a normal teenager. She's seventeen—what do you expect?"

But Sam hadn't heard the anger in Liana's voice just minutes before. Her daughter's harsh words screamed through her mind again. "Leave—me—alone!" Liana had punctuated each word with an intensity that left Joan bewildered and afraid. Then she'd slammed her bedroom door with a frightening ferocity, and the silence flooded in again.

A Mother's Strength

When had the silence begun? Where had her little girl's laughter gone? Where was the sweet sound of her voice as she sang in a backyard swing? Where were the silly secrets that tickled a mother's ear? Replacing the warm sounds of love was an icy silence.

Joan had hoped their upcoming family vacation would provide an opportunity for her and Liana to reconnect. But now she wasn't so sure. She'd been planning the trip to the San Luis Obispo beach for months. Spring break meant the kids would be out of school for a whole week. Her family needed time together—away from all the pressures of their hectic lives.

Joan knew she had an idealistic vision of what the vacation could be. She wanted it to be like the childhood vacation she'd spent there with her family when she was thirteen. It had been her favorite vacation.

The highlight of the trip was when Joan and her mom had spotted a whale. The sky was hazy, and the ocean was gray and choppy. They had been combing the shore for sand dollars when Joan noticed it. It was the biggest thing she'd ever seen. But for all its size, it was graceful and elegant—even playful. "Mom, look! I see a whale! It's . . . it's beautiful."

The Blessing of Silence

Mother and daughter stared out into the vast ocean, eyes glued to the massive creature. As they watched, the gentle beast spewed an enormous geyser of water and plunged into the deep. Joan's heart sank with the whale, and she thought it was gone; but after several long seconds, it resurfaced.

The two of them stood like statues—spellbound—as the majestic mammal glided through the ocean waters. Neither of them said a word. They didn't move. With the sound of the surf in their ears and the cool evening wind blowing on their faces, they watched as time stood still. Finally the great creature turned and, with a thundering splash of its immense tail, swam away.

The next moment was the best of all. Joan had moved to her mother's side and wrapped her arm around her waist. She still remembered her mom's pleasant surprise as she put her arm around Joan and squeezed her tight. They stood side by side in peaceful silence—not needing to say a word. They just smiled and hugged and basked in the warmth of each other's love as they watched the whale disappear into the sea.

Standing outside her angry daughter's door, Joan buried her face in her hands and cried. The wall of silence that separated them was nothing like the peaceful silence she'd shared with her mother those many years ago. What had she done to cause Liana to pull so far away from her? How could she tear down this wall of silence and rebuild their crumbling relationship?

During the drive to the beach, Joan wrestled with her thoughts and prayed. Once there she opened the door of their RV and stepped out. It was as beautiful as she remembered. Joan filled her lungs with the cool, moist air. Her mind swam with visions of the long-ago vacation, but her pleasant memories were abruptly interrupted by Liana's harsh voice.

"I can't believe you brought us here. It's freezing! What a waste of spring break. A whole week on a cold beach."

It was true. It was cold. Cold like their relationship. Cold like the silence that hung between them. This was not the kind of beach where you laid out in the sun. This was the kind of beach where you hiked and explored and discovered. And perhaps . . . rediscovered . . .

Liana's face contorted in disgust. She angrily zipped her blue windbreaker and stuffed her hands in her pockets. "I'm going for a walk. Maybe that'll warm me up."

The Blessing of Silence

Joan watched Liana stomp off, the wall between them growing more real with every step.

After a couple of hours of hard work, Joan and Sam had the campsite set up. "Have you seen Liana?" Joan asked. "She's been gone for over two hours."

"I'm sure she's OK. She probably just needed a little quiet time to herself."

"There's been way too much quiet between the two of us lately. I'm going to find her."

Joan wrapped her jacket tightly around herself and slowly eased into a smile as she walked down the gray beach. The brisk coastal winds whipped through her hair, and she took a long, deep breath. The moist wind was refreshing and invigorating—just like she remembered it. Joan felt as if she were in another world. The busyness of work—gone. The hectic pace of family life—gone. The tensions of strained relationships—Joan remembered the growing tension between her and Liana—not gone. She sighed in resignation and plodded on along the water's edge.

After walking for thirty minutes, Joan began to worry. What if Liana had gotten hurt? What if she was trying to

A Mother's Strength

hitchhike home? What if she'd been kidnapped? Joan quickened her pace. "Liana!" she called. "Liana, where are you?"

Only silence.

Joan strained to see down the coastline. Ahead was a long stretch of sand that seemed to go on forever. If Liana was on the beach, Joan should be able to see at least a speck of her. The vast ocean was to her left, and to her right were tall, rocky cliffs. What if Liana had climbed the cliffs and gotten stuck—or worse, had fallen and was lying alone and unconscious? Joan spotted a pathway that wound up the cliffs. It was the kind of thing that would attract Liana's attention. As a little girl, she'd always been drawn to anything that offered a challenge—anything that seemed to say no.

Joan hurried up the steep path. "Liana!" she called breathlessly. "Liana! Can you hear me?" She stood still and listened as she scanned the cliff. Higher up, Joan thought she saw a flash of blue. "Liana! Is that you?" Again, from behind a clump of trees, she saw the same blue waving but didn't hear a sound. Joan scampered toward the movement. *If that's Liana, what could be keeping her from answering?* Horrible possibilities filled her mind.

The Blessing of Silence

Adrenaline mingled with fear filled Joan with a spurt of energy, and she bounded up the last stretch to the body of trees. With her hand on her chest, she tried to catch her breath. That's when she saw Liana. "Liana! Are you all right? I thought you were hurt." Liana stood on the edge of the cliff with her forefinger to her lips. She was looking intently at something below.

"Shh!" Liana whispered. A mischievous smile played across her face—the first smile Joan had seen on her in months. "Come here," she whispered. Liana waved her mother to her side. "Look!"

Joan crept to the edge and looked down. Below, on a rock platform that jutted from the cliff, was a huge nest made of sticks and twigs and grass. Inside were four pale blue eggs. Much bigger than chicken eggs, they were almost three inches long. "I think they're about to hatch," Liana said excitedly. "I can see them moving, and every now and then I hear a little *cheep* from inside and sometimes a pecking noise." Liana pointed upward. "The mother bird is up there in the tree—watching."

Joan looked up to see a vision from her childhood. It was

a four-foot-tall, blue gray bird with a bright yellow bill and a distinctive S-shaped neck. She patiently watched as her babies struggled to be free of the shells that had nurtured them. "Oh, honey," Joan whispered. "That's a blue heron. It's one of the most amazing birds. When our family came here on vacation, we saw several nests like this in a clump of spruce trees. But we could only see the nests from the ground. We never got to look inside."

Liana and Joan stared at the cheeping, pecking eggs. Suddenly a little beak poked through one of the most active eggs. "Mom, look!" Liana squealed. "It's hatching. It's . . . it's beautiful!" Mother and daughter stood spellbound, transfixed by the miracle of birth. They watched as four baby herons emerged from their shells. Their feathers were wet, and their little eyes opened slowly, adjusting to the light. A couple of them tried to stand, but their wobbly legs collapsed beneath them.

Liana slowly moved to her mother's side and wrapped her arm around her mother's waist. Joan turned to her daughter in surprise, but Liana didn't say a word. She just smiled and squeezed her tightly. Joan put her arm around Liana and returned the squeeze. Mother and daughter stood side by side in peaceful silence—neither needing to say a word. They just smiled and hugged and basked in the warmth of each other's love as they watched the baby birds becoming acquainted with their new world.

This kind of silence, Joan thought, *I don't mind at all.* She looked up at the blue heron above. *If we'll just bide our time, Mama Bird, our babies will find their way.*

3

a mother's lessons

$\mathcal{Y}$ou're unforgettable to Me! I've engraved you on the palms of My hands. Nothing could ever stop Me from loving you. I'll never leave you or let you down. You can love others deeply because true love conceals a multitude of faults.

Hugs,
Your God of Love

—from Isaiah 49:16; Romans 8:38–39;
Deuteronomy 31:6; 1 Peter 4:8

Life forever teaches, and mothers are forever learning. And sometimes our most important lessons come from our children.

Let's be honest. A mother's life isn't always easy. Even though we try to be super moms and super friends and super citizens and super wives, we don't always do it perfectly. Not only are we highly invested in the lives of our children, we are also intricately intertwined with in-laws, siblings, parents, friends, and husbands. And sometimes our relationships with others can get complicated. Unfortunately, our children witness our relationship failures as well as our successes.

Children see and hear things that belie our teaching. Their little radar is highly tuned to the relationships between the people they love and depend on. And when those relationships slip, the simple honesty of our children's hearts may be just what we need to bring us back to what we know is true.

A wise mother keeps her radar tuned to the hearts of her children and to the lessons waiting to be unearthed there. Observing how a child dawdles joyfully on a walk around the block teaches us to slow down and enjoy a long cup of coffee with the husband with whom we've grown impatient. Sharing in the wonder of a child discovering tadpoles encourages us to discover new treasures in the lives of old friends. And experiencing the purity of the love in a child's embrace opens our hearts to the possibility of rebuilding a love we thought was lost.

No one who has ever brought up a child
can doubt for a moment that love
is literally the life-giving fluid
of human existence.

Smiley Blanton

If they could forget
that they loved each
other, maybe they
could forget that
they loved her and
Robbie too.

Forgotten Love

Meagan clutched the silver frame to her chest. This was her only chance. If this didn't work, she didn't know what she'd do.

She seemed to be the only one in her family who remembered. Well, maybe Robbie remembered, but he was too little to understand. He was only three. She was bigger—much bigger. She was five.

Meagan had convinced her mom, Marianne, to let her go through the cashier's line by herself. "I'm using my Barbie money, Mom, and I don't want you to see which Barbie till we get home." Under normal circumstances her mom would have asked a million questions: Why don't you want me to

A Mother's Lessons

see? Are you sure you have enough money? Do you remember how to count your change? But today—and for the last few days—her mom had been distracted, her mind on other things.

Meagan understood. Her mind had been on other things too.

Meagan thought back to the fight she'd overheard three nights ago. Her mom and dad hadn't known she was listening. But she'd heard every word. And peeking through the open crack of her bedroom door, she'd seen what they did.

She'd never heard her mom and dad talk like that before. They were angry and mean; they were yelling—loud. Her mother had gotten so mad that she threw their wedding picture across the room. It hit the wall and crashed to the floor. The glass shattered into tiny pieces, and the pretty silver frame broke apart. Then her mom had grabbed the picture off the floor and ripped it in half. "I've had it!" she yelled. "It's over. This marriage is over!"

Meagan's dad had stomped toward the door, yelling, "Fine! I'm outta here! I'm sick and tired of your criticizing my every move. I can't do anything right! I don't know why I even try!" Then he stormed out the door and slammed it behind him. Meagan heard the car start and knew her daddy was gone.

Meagan's mom crumpled to the floor, sobbing as she fell. She picked up the broken picture frame and tried to put it back together again, but it was no use. It was bent and broken—irreparable. She swept up the broken glass and put the pieces of the frame and torn picture inside the entertainment-center cabinet. "I'm better off forgetting you," she whispered as she walked sadly to her room. But she turned as she closed her bedroom door and looked longingly at the cabinet. New tears rolled down her cheeks.

After her mom went to bed, Meagan tiptoed to the cabinet, opened the door, and gathered the remnants of her parents' forgotten love. She carried them reverently back to her room and put them under her bed in her secret box. She didn't know what she was going to do with them, but she knew they couldn't stay in the cabinet—forgotten.

Meagan's dad had been out of work for six months. Her mom's job at the bank wasn't enough to pay all the bills, and when there wasn't enough money, they both got grumpy. But that night they'd been more than grumpy. Much more. Never before had her mom and dad yelled at each other.

A Mother's Lessons

They loved each other—Meagan was sure of it. And they loved her too, and her little brother, Robbie.

But they seemed to have forgotten their love. And if they could forget that they loved each other, maybe they could forget that they loved her and Robbie too. Meagan was scared. She had to make her mom remember.

"Please put my frame in a bag you can't see through," Meagan said politely to the woman behind the counter. "It's a surprise for my mommy."

"She'll *love* it," the woman whispered kindly.

Meagan stood on her tiptoes and leaned toward the woman. "I hope it will help her remember to love *Daddy*," she whispered back.

When she got home, Meagan dashed to her room and closed the door. She laid her purchase on the bed and retrieved her secret box. Meagan pulled out the torn photo. She got the Scotch tape she'd stashed in her drawer and climbed onto her bed. She scooted to the center so she'd have plenty of room to work. First she carefully matched the torn pieces of the photo and taped them along the front and the back so they'd be sure to stay where they belonged—together. Then she opened the back of the new frame, like she'd seen Nana do when Meagan gave her a new picture. She placed the repaired photo facedown on the glass, then replaced the cardboard and closed the clasps. "There!" she said as she turned it around for inspection. "Please remember." Meagan carefully placed the frame back in the bag and slid it under her bed.

That night at dinner, Meagan, Robbie, and their mother ate the usual Saturday-night meatloaf, and then they had banana pudding for dessert—just like they had done every Saturday night for as long as they could remember. But something was missing from their weekend routine. Daddy. It was time to put her plan into action.

"Mommy, do you remember the day I was born?"

"It was one of the best days of my life. My mother was there, Nana was there—Aunt Rachel too."

"Was Daddy there, Mommy?"

"Yes, Daddy was there too."

"Do you remember when I learned to walk?"

"Meagan, you've heard me tell this story a hundred times."

"I know, but I want to hear it again."

"Oh, all right. Well, your daddy and I had been on a trip. We went to Gatlinburg, Tennessee. It was so beautiful. Your dad planned the whole trip without telling me—a surprise for my birthday . . ." Her eyes got a faraway look in them—a happy look.

"When we got home, you were so excited to see us that you walked for the first time—back and forth between me and Daddy." She shook away the memories and looked at Meagan. "Enough remembering. Let's clear this table."

"Wait, Mommy. I have a surprise for you."

"I want to see Mommy's 'prise," Robbie squealed. "I want to see!"

"OK, Robbie, you can see too. Just wait a minute," Meagan insisted.

"You have a surprise for *me?*" their mother asked incredulously.

"Yes—close your eyes, and I'll get it." Meagan ran to her room and returned with her hands behind her back. "OK, you can open your eyes now."

As her mom opened her eyes, Meagan produced the brown paper bag. "Here, Mommy. This is to help you remember."

"Help me remember?" she asked as she pulled the gift from the bag. "Help me remember what?"

She turned the frame around and gasped. Her eyes filled with tears, and she put her hand to her mouth.

"Meagan, how did you—where did you get—"

"I bought it with my Barbie money."

"You spent your Barbie money on this frame—for me? It's beautiful."

"It's to help you remember, Mommy. To help you remember the day you and Daddy got married—to help you remember that you love Daddy. I know you do. I saw you crying the night he left, and I remember how you and Daddy used to hug and laugh. I remember that you love each other. Can you remember, Mommy? Try real hard. Can you remember?"

A stout knock at the front door interrupted Meagan's pleading.

While her mother sat stunned, Meagan ran to the front door, flipped on the porch light, and stood on her tiptoes to look out the window. "It's Daddy!" she squealed. She flung open the door and threw herself into his arms. "Did you remember, Daddy? Did you remember?"

"Remember what?" he said as he placed her gently back on the floor.

A Mother's Lessons

"Did you remember that you love Mommy?"

Marianne walked quietly over to her husband. She held out the mended photo in the new frame. "Meagan is trying to help me remember the day we married, so I can remember that I love you."

Understanding dawned on his face. He took the photo, tears filling his eyes too. "Did you fix the picture, Meagan?"

"Yes. I fixed it for you and Mommy. And I bought a new frame with my Barbie money. I thought that if you remembered your wedding day, you would remember your love."

"I think I do remember," he said, looking into Marianne's glistening eyes. He slipped his arm around his wife's waist, and she allowed him to pull her to him.

"I remember too, Robert. It was the happiest day of my life."

Marianne and Robert opened their embrace to allow room for Robbie and Meagan. "Come here, you two," Marianne said, "I think we'll all remember this moment for a very long time."

4

a mother's words

words

$\mathcal{D}$iscover joy in the midst of life's daily struggles, knowing that the testing of your faith is building perseverance. When you ask Me, I'll generously give you wisdom for the circumstances confronting you and your family.

Guiding you,
Your Heavenly Father

—from James 1:2–5

When you were a child, you probably learned the adage "Sticks and stones may break my bones, but words can never hurt me." It was used to minimize the damage of hurtful words or to cut the insult slinger down to size. But no matter how many times you said it, you knew it wasn't true. Words can hurt us deeply.

Yet words also have the power to heal. Words of kindness are a salve on a wounded spirit. Words of assurance can take the sting out of defeat. Words of love instill a sense of wholeness and well-being that can withstand life's harshest winds. Your words, Mom, are some of the most potent in the world, for they're born of years of loving and knowing your child. Your words have the power to help and heal.

The bond you share with your child is like none other. Though mysterious and intangible, it is the fruit of simple, everyday interactions. Like holding hands and kissing hurts, reading stories and rocking late at night, listening to silly chatter and cheering little accomplishments. This bond grows and ripens through the years, and from it comes a kind of knowing, a sensing, a cognizance of your child's deepest needs. This bond gives you insight into *what* your child needs to hear and *when*.

Maybe we need to change that old adage to reflect the power of a mother's words: Life is tough and sometimes rough, but

*T*each your children to
think things through for themselves
at an early age, so they will know how to
make the tough decisions later on when
you're not around.

Paul Faulkner

Miriam did look stunning. But Lori wasn't at all confident that this marriage would make all of Miriam's dreams come true.

Wedding Bells

Lori Marshall's daughter looked like a princess straight out of a fairy tale. Lori adjusted the big bow on the back of Miriam's white satin bodice and stepped back to take a look. "Oh, sweetheart, you look wonderful. I can't believe my baby is getting married. You're going to make a beautiful bride."

"I love it, Mom," Miriam said, her face beaming. "The taffeta skirt makes me feel like Cinderella."

The dress was indeed beautiful, and Miriam did look stunning. But Lori wasn't at all confident that this marriage would make all of Miriam's dreams come true. Markus certainly didn't fit Lori's dreams for her only daughter. There wasn't anything really *bad* about him, but there wasn't anything especially good either.

"They did a great job of adjusting the bodice. It's perfect!" Miriam was delighted. Lori tried to look happy.

Miriam was a bright, passionate young woman, and Markus was . . . well, without aspiration. Lori knew that love could bring out the best in people, but her heart told her that Miriam wasn't really in love with Markus. At times,Lori was afraid Miriam was more in love with the *idea* of being in love than she was with the man she was about to marry. As a little girl, she'd always loved stories of beautiful princesses who married handsome princes and lived happily ever after. The romance, the whirl, the fantasy, the excitement—that's what Miriam loved.

"Let's try on your veil to make sure the headpiece fits," Lori suggested valiantly.

The wedding was only three weeks away. The bridesmaids' dresses were due to come in tomorrow. The caterer had been reserved. The flowers had been commissioned, and invitations had been sent.

"Thank you, Mom," Miriam said, giving Lori a big hug.

Wedding Bells

"You're the best. You've been so supportive through all this. I love you!"

You wouldn't think I was so supportive if you knew what I was thinking. Lori silently returned her daughter's smile. She had spent hours thinking and praying about how she should handle her misgivings about Markus. She had watched her older sister, Janice, criticize and bemoan her daughter's choice of a husband. The marriage had taken place in spite of her protests, and the relationship between mother and daughter had suffered terribly—not to mention the damage it did to Janice's relationship with her new son-in-law.

Miriam was an independent, strong-willed girl. Lori knew that butting heads with her would result only in hurt feelings and perhaps long-term damage. Miriam was also extremely intelligent and introspective. Given enough time, Lori believed she would see the truth herself. She just hoped they had enough time.

Lori's misgivings had begun the weekend she and Miriam discussed wedding music. She had driven the four hours south to her daughter's college to help with wedding plans. They'd had a great time looking through catalogs and talking about flowers, but when Lori suggested that Miriam and Markus needed to start planning their music, Miriam had balked.

"I don't need Markus to plan the music, Mom. You can help me." So Lori dug out all the tapes of wedding music she'd brought and planned to leave with Miriam, and they began listening. Lori remembered choosing her own wedding music with her husband-to-be. She had been so excited. The music had been so romantic! Every song expressed their love in a different way. But nothing seemed to stir Miriam. If she did get excited about a song, the reason was never Markus. It was the beautiful words or the orchestra or even a memory of a fun date with someone else.

"Honey, haven't any of these songs expressed how you feel about Markus?"

"We just haven't found the right one yet, Mom. We need to keep listening."

But Lori knew that her question had given expression to something deep inside of Miriam and that her words had resonated in her daughter's heart.

And so, over the months of wedding preparation, Lori had asked gentle questions she hoped would help her daughter figure things out for herself. As often as was appropriate, she reminded her of what she'd taught her all her life: "Up until the second you say *I do*, you can back out at any time; but after that your whole heart needs to be committed 'until death do you part.'" But lately she'd been adding, "I mean it, honey—no matter how much money we've spent or how many plans we've laid. If you ever feel this marriage is not what you want, you just say the word. It'll be OK."

As Lori and Miriam drove home from the fitting, Lori chatted about housing plans for all the relatives who'd be coming in for the wedding. "Miriam, I don't think you've heard a word I've said," Lori pressed softly. "What are you thinking about?"

"Oh, I was just thinking about Markus. He invited me to come stay the weekend at his parents' house."

"Well, that's nice, sweetie. It'll be good for you and Markus to have some time together. You and I have been so busy with wedding plans that I'll bet he's missing you. Plus it'll be a good time to get to know his parents better."

"But I don't really want to go. I'd rather stay home."

"Why, honey? Is it that you don't want to spend time with his parents?"

A Mother's Words

"No, it's more like I don't want to spend time with Markus."

Everything in Lori told her that now was the time to say something, the time to help Miriam ask questions she should be asking herself.

"Well, Miriam, if you don't want to spend time with Markus, why are you marrying him?"

"I don't know, Mom. I don't think I want to."

"You don't want to what, Miriam?"

"I don't want to marry Markus!"

Lori pulled the car over to the side of the road and brought it to a stop. "I don't want you to marry him either!" Miriam fell into her mother's arms, and they hugged hard and long.

"How did you figure out that you didn't want to marry Markus?"

"I guess it was all your questions. You helped me consider things I wasn't able to think about on my own. But you did it in a way that didn't make me feel threatened or pushed. You of all people know I don't like to be pushed."

Lori smiled. She did know. "You're such a smart young woman. I knew you'd figure it out given enough time."

Wedding Bells

Miriam wiped the tears from her cheeks and smiled. "I feel so much better now. I feel like a huge burden has been lifted. I hadn't realized it, but this wedding thing has become a dreadful weight on my heart. I feel free!"

Miriam's face registered a troubling thought. "But, Mom, what about poor Markus? This is going to *crush* him."

"I know, sweetheart. It will be hard on him. But you're making the right decision—I'm sure of it."

"Oh, and Mom! What about the wedding dress? What about the flowers and the caterer? What about the invitations? We've already sent them!"

"What have I told you all your life?"

"That once I say *I do*, I need to commit with all my heart."

"What's the *other* thing I always say?"

"That *until* I say *I do*, it's never too late to call off a wedding. But Mom, you and Dad have spent so much money. We have relatives coming from all over the country. All my bridesmaids have had their dresses fitted. Everything is planned!"

"None of that matters in light of the life you have ahead of you. We take marriage seriously in our family, and I don't want you to get married until it's to someone you want to spend your whole life with."

"I think I've known for a while now that Markus wasn't the one, but it was so hard to admit that I'd made such a serious mistake. It's great to know that my family loves me, no matter what."

"I do love you, princess. I'm just glad you figured this out before your enchanted carriage turned into a pumpkin. Your handsome prince is out there somewhere just waiting to discover you—just waiting to make your dreams come true."

5

a mother's love

love

$\mathcal{L}$ove is the greatest gift! Nothing compares to My unfailing love for you. Even before you were born, I was thinking of you. I know you personally and call you by name. My hand will guide you and hold you—always!

Loving you today and always,
Your Heavenly Father

—from 1 Corinthians 13:13; Ephesians 3:18–19; Psalm 139:10, 16

71

A mother's love is like the powers of Superman. It can leap tall obstacles in a single bound, racing with help and support for a child in distress. It's more powerful than a locomotive, pressing past difficulties and enduring hardship for the sake of a troubled child. It's faster than a speeding bullet, flying swiftly to the side of a son or daughter in need.

But there's one significant difference between the power of a mother's love and those of Superman: Superman's powers are fantasy. A mother's love is real.

A mother's love is born even before her child is. As she anticipates the new arrival, she falls in love with a child she has yet to know. And when she holds that child for the first time, she knows that the bond between them is sealed forever.

Personal limitations are pushed aside when it comes to a child's needs. For the sake of her offspring, she'll attempt things she thought were impossible or tasks she's feared her whole life. Trepidation turns to strength, fear to hope, and sadness finds a new kind of joy.

The next time you hear "It's a bird; it's a plane; it's Superman!" you'll know in your heart that no superhero can compare with the very real power of a mother's love.

Give a little love to a child,
and you get a great deal back.

John Ruskin

Though she had never

seen these qualities

in the eyes of anyone

who had ever looked

at her, she recognized

them right away.

Don't Call Me Mommy

Charlotte straightened her hat and turned to look over the rows of people behind her. *Where's Jacob?* she wondered. *He was supposed to be here ten minutes ago.* A queasy feeling gripped her stomach. *Calm down, Charlotte,* she said to herself. *This is the easy part.* It had taken Charlotte a long time to get where she was tonight. The journey had been the hard part.

Charlotte's mother was the kind of woman most people see only on TV. "Quit screaming, you stupid kid!" Charlotte could still hear her mother's voice, still feel the sting of her mother's hand across her face. She remembered her own hand flying to her wounded cheek. She remembered looking

A Mother's Love

in bewilderment into her mother's bloodshot eyes. Her mother's face was swollen and red, her hair, dry and matted. But what Charlotte remembered most was her mother's voice—and her words. "How could you be so *dumb?*" Her words had been filled with a contempt that four-year-old Charlotte couldn't understand but could certainly feel. "You'll never amount to anything. A kid like you never learns. You're *stupid*. You'll always be stupid." Charlotte had cried as her heart felt a pain far worse than that inflicted by her mother's hand.

"Mommy," Charlotte had pleaded, "Why are you so mad at me? I love you, Mommy. I love you."

Her mother had raised her hand again. "Quit whining, I told you. And don't call me Mommy."

A few days later, a man and a woman from social services had come to get her. When Charlotte refused to go with them, the woman had simply scooped her up.

"Put me down! Put me down! I want my mommy!" Charlotte had screamed and kicked—she even bit the woman's arm—but the woman was too strong, and her mother didn't try to stop her. "Mommy, don't let them take me. Please, Mommy, I'll be good. I won't cry anymore."

Don't Call Me Mommy

But her mother had turned away. "Quit whining, you stupid kid. When will you understand that I don't want you. And stop calling me Mommy."

That was the last time Charlotte had seen her mother—yet she had spent a lifetime trying to forget those words and that face.

Her mother's words shaped Charlotte's life. She *hadn't* been smart. School had been more than difficult for her. Every time she took a test or wrote a paper, she proved her mother right.

She proved her mother right again when she married Jimmy. When Charlotte was seventeen, she met Jimmy at the convenience store where he'd worked since dropping out of high school. He was cocky and bold, and Charlotte had liked that because she was anything *but* bold. They got married two weeks after her high-school graduation.

Jimmy drank away every bit of money he made at the convenience store, and it wasn't long before he began hitting her. She was so stupid she couldn't even figure out how to leave him. Jimmy figured it out for her when she got pregnant. "You stupid idiot! How could you get pregnant? I told you I don't want kids." When Charlotte started crying, his anger only intensified. "Get out of my sight! You're stupid, Charlotte, stupid! Leave, I said—get out of here!"

Charlotte had stumbled down the dark stairwell of their ramshackle apartment building and into the even darker night. All she had was what she was wearing—the grease-stained uniform from the restaurant where she worked. She had in her possession only one thing that mattered: the baby that was growing inside her.

She gave birth in a home for unwed mothers, and then she and little Jacob moved into a subsidized apartment. Jacob went to a state-funded daycare center while she worked at Dairy Barn, serving ice cream and hamburgers to people who looked at her like she was stupid. And she was sure they were right.

There was only one person in the whole world who didn't seem to think she was stupid, only one person who saw anything good in her. When she looked into the eyes of her precious baby, she saw no hint of the contempt she'd seen in her mother's eyes or in Jimmy's. Instead, she saw trust and confidence—and something more—she saw love. Though she had never seen these qualities in the eyes of anyone who had ever looked at her, she recognized them right away; and they filled her heart with a hope she'd never known.

And so Charlotte had determined to learn one thing. She was certain she was incapable of anything else, but surely she could learn how to be Jacob's mother. And so she set out to learn. She read books on parenting and took parenting classes at the YWCA. She watched how other mothers parented their children—not the bad kind, but the kind who smiled and told their children that they were smart; the kind who let their children call them Mommy.

And she learned. And on the way to learning how to be a mother, she learned other things too. She took a vocational course to learn how to work in an office. After earning her diploma, she got a job in a law office, answering phones and filing papers. She worked hard and in two years was promoted to office manager.

When she picked up Jacob from school, she would smile at him and tell him how smart he was. She'd tell him she loved him. And she loved it when he called her Mommy.

The afternoon Jacob had announced that he was going to college was an afternoon that changed Charlotte's life—again. "Oh, Jacob. I am so proud of you. I always wanted to go to college, but it just didn't work out. Besides, I'm not nearly as smart as you. I could never make it in college. I barely got out of high school."

"What are you talking about, Mom?" her handsome son asked. "You're one of the smartest people I know. You always know just the right thing to say to me when I'm discouraged. You know how to make the best chocolate cake in the world, and you know everything there is to know about every sport I ever played. Mom, you can learn anything you set your mind to."

"No, Jacob. I do those things because I love you. It doesn't take any brains to love a child like you."

"Mom." Jacob put his hands on Charlotte's shoulders and turned her to meet his strong gaze. His voice was deep and full of conviction. "What is it you'd like to learn? If you went to college, what would you do with your education?"

Charlotte looked over her son's shoulder at the ceiling as she contemplated the question she had asked herself countless times in the last eighteen years. "That's easy. I would be a child advocate in the court system. I'd help children whose mothers don't love them. I would love children whose mothers don't want to be called Mommy."

Jacob pulled his mother to him and hugged her then suddenly pulled away. "Mom, I have the best idea!"

"What?"

"Mom, I want you to go to college when I do."

Charlotte shook her head in instant protest, but Jacob talked all the more excitedly. "You can do this, Mom, I'm absolutely sure you can."

So that's how Charlotte came to be sitting in the gymnasium of Westbury College, adjusting her cap and smoothing the fabric of her blue graduation gown. The empty seat beside her was Jacob's. *Come on, son. If you don't get here soon, you're going to miss your own graduation—and mine too.*

Charlotte turned once more to scan the doors at the back of the auditorium. There he was! Smiling broadly, Jacob strode down the aisle wearing the blue cap and gown that matched his mother's. Charlotte waved excitedly.

She made her way to the aisle, stepping over toes and offering apologies. "Jacob, I thought you'd never get here! What took you so long?"

"I had to stop off and get something."

"Whatever could you need so badly that you'd almost be late to your own graduation?" It was then that she noticed that Jacob had his hand behind his back. "What do you have back there?"

"It's something for a special grad," he said with a mischievous sparkle in his dark brown eyes. With a flourish, Jacob whipped his arm from behind his back and produced the biggest bunch of red roses Charlotte had ever seen. "For you, Mom," Jacob said proudly.

"Oh, Jacob. You are too good to be true." Charlotte smiled as she dabbed at a tear. "No one has ever given me flowers before. Thank you."

"Come on, Mom, don't get all mushy on me. You're going to make us late to our graduation."

Halfway through the speaker's presentation, Charlotte noticed a card tucked down in the roses. She pulled it out of its envelope. "To the smartest person I know. Thanks for letting me call you Mommy."

There was no stopping the tears now. Charlotte squeezed her son's hand and whispered in his ear. "I love you, son. Don't ever stop calling me Mommy."

6

a mother's vision

vision

*Y*ou can always count on Me. My love and faithfulness will endure for all generations. When you love Me and are called according to My purposes, you can trust Me to transform even the hard things into blessings for your family. Let Me be your stronghold in times of trouble.

Faithfully,
Your God of Purpose

—from Psalm 100:5; Romans 8:28; Psalm 37:39

$\mathcal{A}$ mother can see what's not there and imagine the improbable. Her sight isn't bound by earthly boundaries, for its source is not of this world. Empowered by heaven, a mother's eyes can see beyond the immediate and into the potential. A mother's eyes dream of possibilities and expect a promise.

Not everything in a mother's life is as she'd hoped. Life dishes out disappointments as well as dreams. It metes out maladies as well as marvels. It's easy to envision victory when you're on a winning streak. It's in the face of defeat that a mother's eyes really shine. When finances restrict, when relationships fall apart, when the road ends and no new path opens up—this is when a mother must will herself to visualize something fresh, something better, something beyond.

Sometimes what disappoints is not life's circum-stances but the child you love. Innocent babies are sometimes born with disabling deformities. Teenagers turn from truths you've taught their whole lives. Adult children make choices that not only impair their own lives but tragically affect your own. But your eyes still see hope, they forever envision possibilities.

What is it that makes this transforming vision possible? It's love. Love that looks into the eyes of a misshapen child and sees an angel. Love that when faced with a shattered life, sees a shin-ing light. Love cannot be squelched; it cannot be annihilated. Love is the greatest of earthly emotions. And love will see you home.

A clear vision cuts a mighty path
through obstacles.

Joe Aldrich

Missy stared in disbelief at the vision before her. "What's wrong with my baby's face?"

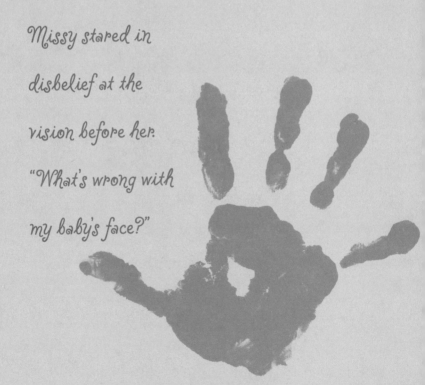

A Normal Little Girl

Sitting in the hospital bed, Missy stared down at the tiny pink bundle in her arms. Little bubbles formed on Mia's delicate mouth, and the baby looked up at her mother for the first time. Her eyes were wide open and full of softness. She blinked gently as she adjusted to the light. *She almost looks normal*, Missy thought as she stroked Mia's pink skin.

Missy looked up into the eyes of her husband, Jason. They didn't reflect the confidence she'd come to count on.

"Come on, dear, give your baby a little kiss," the nurse said. Her patronizing tone made Missy bristle.

Missy wanted to tell this condescending nurse that this was her *third* child, that she *knew* how to be a mother, and

A Mother's Vision

that she *did* love her little girl. But before she could reply, Missy's mind flashed back to the day she learned her baby girl wasn't going to be the normal, healthy child she'd expected. When she'd run into her friend Beverly after coming from the doctor's office, Beverly had patted Missy's tummy and gushed, "I know you just can't wait for that little girl to be born." Missy had smiled and nodded her head, but in her heart she whispered, *I can wait.*

Maybe the nurse was right. Maybe she didn't know how to be a mother to the baby in her arms.

Her doubts about her ability to mother this baby had taken root the day of her second ultrasound. Her doctor's office had a new ultrasound machine that promised a clearer, more detailed image. Missy waited excitedly as the nurse spread the cold gel on her abdomen. Soon the image of the baby began to appear. Thirty-one-week-old Mia was turned so her back was toward Missy. In awe, Missy studied the curve of her spine and counted ten little fingers and ten little toes. *Turn around, little one,* she willed baby Mia to turn. *Let Mommy see your pretty little face.* Right before her eyes, little Mia turned as if she'd heard and understood her mother's voice. But when Missy saw her baby's face, her eyes widened in shock. She let out a small scream as she put her hand to her mouth.

Missy stared in disbelief at the vision before her. Surely she was imagining what she thought she saw. "What is it?" Missy asked, her voice trembling. "What's wrong with my baby's face?"

For the next few days, Missy did little but cry. She cried for what she had lost: she cried for the loss of her expectations, for the loss of her dreams, for the loss of a beautiful, normal little girl.

But after a time, Missy turned her attention to learning about Mia's condition. She searched Internet sites and talked to other families who had children with similar abnormalities. She began to understand the terms *cleft lip* and *cleft palate*. She learned the difference between a complete and incomplete cleft. She discovered that the most difficult abnormality to repair in Mia's condition was a cleft palate—when the roof of the mouth is split, in addition to the split in the upper lip. Doctors couldn't be sure which of the conditions Mia had—or how severe they'd be—until she was born.

Now, looking down at her baby, Missy believed she

might be "normal." But her daydream was broken by the concerned whispers of two nurses in the corner. One of them came and stood by Missy's bed, looking intently at Mia for several seconds. Missy's stomach began to roll, and her heart pounded. Something wasn't right—something more than the obvious.

"Your baby is having some difficulty breathing," the nurse said with measured calm. "We need to take her to the NICU to check her out. Don't worry. We just need to make sure everything's OK."

But Missy *was* worried. "Jason? What's going on? Why do they want to take Mia?"

"It'll be OK, honey. We knew she might have some difficulty breathing because of the facial problems. They're just being careful."

Missy watched wistfully as the nurse took Mia and disappeared into the corridor, Jason following protectively behind. "Take care of my baby," Missy whispered to the closing door.

Panic gripped Missy's heart. Her throat felt tight, and fear rose in her chest. Her baby was having trouble breathing! What if she didn't make it? Would she have to go home with empty arms? All the unhappiness she'd felt over Mia's deformity now flooded her with guilt. *I was worried that I wouldn't have the perfect baby. Now I may have no baby at all. Oh, please, God, send Your angels to watch over my little angel. Please let her live.*

At that moment all the months of grieving transformed into an overwhelming love for her misshapen blessing. *Thank You, God, for Mia. Please be with her right now. No matter how many surgeries lie ahead, no matter how many scars remain—I want that child, Father. I want her in our lives.*

The panic she'd felt just moments before was replaced with a peace that outmatched the reality she faced. She knew this calm was heaven-sent. Missy relaxed against her pillows. *Thank You, God. Thank You for being with my baby when I can't be.*

As Missy lay alone in her hospital bed, her thoughts turned to her two sons—five-year-old Cole and eight-year-old Reed. What would they think of little Mia? How would her sons learn to look beyond her face to see the angel residing in their little sister? Missy prayed that Mia would live long enough for her brothers to "see" her beauty.

Just then Jason burst into the room. Missy sat up straight,

every muscle at attention. "How is she, Jason? What's happening? Is she going to be OK?"

Trying to catch his breath, Jason said, "She's going to be all right, Missy! I just talked to the doctor. The breathing difficulties had nothing to do with her facial abnormalities. She has wet lungs, a condition that affects many C-section babies." He hugged Missy reassuringly. "She's going to be OK!"

Missy sank back into her bed. *Thank You, God. Thank You for taking care of my little angel.*

"What about her face, Jason?" It was the question she knew she had to ask. "How bad is it?"

"It's pretty bad." Jason spoke solemnly. "She has one complete cleft . . ."

Missy sucked in her breath.

"The other one is incomplete."

"What about her palate?" Missy asked, dreading the answer but with more confidence than she'd felt since viewing Mia's face on the ultrasound monitor eight weeks earlier.

"She has a partially split palate." Jason looked at Missy to gauge her reaction. He seemed reassured by what he saw.

"I'm OK, Jason." Missy was surprised at the serenity she felt. "I really am. When I thought Mia might die, her facial distortions became insignificant. I just wanted her to live."

Missy's thoughts returned to her two boys who waited at home with their grandma. "Jason, how are we going to help the boys understand what a precious gift Mia is? I know the surgeries will eventually correct her deformities, but I want them to see the beauty in her as she is right now. How are we going to teach them to love her just as she is?"

Jason took Missy's hand and looked into her eyes, his old confidence obviously returning. "They'll find their way with her. Once we get her home and they're able to spend some time with her, they'll find their way."

One week later mother and baby were home and settling into a routine. Missy was learning how to feed her baby in spite of her split lip and palate, and the boys were getting used to having a little sister around. One afternoon Missy sent Cole to check on the sleeping Mia. "What's she doing, Cole?" Missy asked as he raced back into the kitchen.

"She's sleeping. And she's doing *this*." He held up two fingers and placed them over his lips, pointing up toward his nose. "I don't mean she's *doing* this; I mean she *looks* like this."

Missy put down her dishtowel and knelt so she could be

A Mother's Vision

eye to eye with her five-year-old. "I know what you mean, sweetie." Missy took a deep breath and continued. "Let's get your brother. We need to talk."

Missy took Cole by the hand and walked him into the living room where Reed was playing. "Boys, come sit by me for a minute." Missy sat on the couch with Cole by her side and Reed on the floor. Reed looked up at her quizzically. "What is it, Mommy? Is something wrong with Mia?"

"No, nothing's wrong with Mia." Missy paused and took another breath. "Boys, I want to ask you something."

"What, Mommy?" Cole asked, still and quiet for the first time all day.

"I know your sister doesn't look like other little babies. I know she's not quite *normal*. But I want to know—what do you think of your little sister?"

Cole tilted his head up, and a serious, thoughtful expression came over his face. "Well, I thought she was going to look yuck. But she doesn't. She's really kind of pretty."

Missy smiled broadly and turned to Reed.

"What about you, Reed, what do you think?" Reed took his time in answering, as if measuring his eight-year-old words. "I've been thinking about her, Mom, and you know what I think?"

Missy held her breath.

"I was thinking we should change her name."

"What should we change it to?" Missy asked with some trepidation.

"I was thinking we could call her Angel."

Relieved and full of gratitude and love, Missy wrapped both boys in her arms. "Mia is too little right now to understand what awesome big brothers she has. But she's going to understand one day. She's a blessed little girl."

Missy squeezed her boys tightly and smiled again. *Who needs normal*, Missy thought, *when you can have an angel instead?*

7

a mother's joy

$\mathcal{I}$ am with you no matter where you are. Let Me satisfy you each morning with My unfailing love. Be glad! I've shown you the path of life. Let My presence fill you with joy. Stay by My side and experience eternal pleasures.

Shining on you,
Your Joyful God

—from Joshua 1:9; Psalms 90:14; 16:11

Joy is a state of mind before it's a feeling. It grows out of the way we see the world.

True joy originates in our ability to see the world through God's eyes. God sees the truth of things—the good and the bad—and yet is filled with joy. A mother's joy is rooted in a trust in God. Not trust that everything will turn out as she desires—for it may not. Not trust that her children's lives will be easy—they likely will not be. But trust that God loves her children even more than she does. And though He won't force His will upon them, He'll offer them a way and a place in Him.

Joy doesn't eliminate sadness

and grief; it doesn't protect from disappointment or fear. But it can coexist with the sad things of life, for it wells up from deep inside your soul; it grows in the fertile soil of hope.

When life brings you to a new place, a new role, a new time; when your job as a mother changes—hold on to your joy. As our children grow and find their place in this world, hold on to your joy. You have new tasks to apply it to, new people to share it with. You'll find that with time, your joy will resurface in the lives of your children as they make homes of their own—homes filled with their mother's joy.

We leave traces of ourselves
wherever we go, on whatever we touch.

Lewis Thomas

She knew it was time

for her boys to live

lives of their own.

But she didn't like

it one bit.

A New Start

The sound of the spraying water and the feel of the cool mist calmed Alesa's distressed spirit. It had been three months since her baby boy went off to college. She'd always stayed home with her boys, so now that the last of her four sons was gone, her days seemed long and empty.

Alesa directed the spray nozzle to the next rose bush. Her roses were the best in the neighborhood. Years of carefully tending them had taught her when to prune, when to feed, and how often to water. But today she could barely keep her mind on her tasks. She knew that children were supposed to grow up and leave home. She knew that one of the goals of mothering was to create independent adults. And she knew

A Mother's Joy

it was time for her boys to live lives of their own. She knew all of that. And she believed it to be true. But she didn't like it one bit.

She had her gardening, of course, but a garden was a poor substitute for a child. Alesa turned her attention to her hydrangea bushes. She tenderly broke off any dead blooms and inspected the leaves for signs of insects. *Children are like plants*, she thought. *They're so fragile, yet amazingly resilient. You have to know when to prune their adventurous spirits and when to let them grow unhindered. They're a lot of trouble— needing constant attention and care—yet they provide such joy.*

Her ruminations were interrupted by a tug on her sleeve. A little girl stood by her side, looking up at her with big, blue eyes. "Do you have any children?" she asked.

"Well, yes I do, but they're all grown. They don't live here anymore."

The child's disappointed face mirrored the disappointment in Alesa's heart. "Do you know where some kids live?" the girl asked. "We just moved in the yellow house down the street, and I don't have anyone to play with."

Alesa thought for a minute. "I can't think of any your age. Most are older, like my boys, grown and gone."

A New Start

Big tears threatened to spill from the child's brilliant eyes.

"My name is Mrs. Woodham," Alesa said, trying to distract her new friend. "What's yours?"

"I'm Ellie. I have a brother, but he's too big. He never plays with me. I don't even have a mommy." At this revelation tears fell from her eyes and onto the moist soil below.

Alesa bent down so she was eye level with Ellie. "Ellie, how would you like to help me water my garden? Working in my garden always makes me feel better." Alesa produced a crisp, clean tissue from her pocket. "Here, wipe those tears on this. I keep some handy for when I get sad."

That got Ellie's attention. "Why do *you* get sad?"

"Well, you know how you get sad because your mommy isn't with you anymore? I get sad because my children aren't with me. So I guess we have something in common."

A smile spread across Ellie's face, and she eagerly took the watering can Alesa held out to her. "These flowers are very thirsty. Do you think you can give them a drink? Make sure the dirt they're growing in gets good and wet."

Ellie set about her task with serious intent. "Did your children die?"

"No, they just moved away to start their own lives."

A Mother's Joy

"My mommy died," Ellie said. "She died when I was five, but I'm big now. I'm six. We moved here so my daddy could have a new job. He says it's a new start. But I liked our old start better."

"That's what my husband calls this time in our lives without children—a new start. But I'm with you. I like the old start better too."

Alesa and Ellie watered side by side, Alesa stopping to fill Ellie's watering can whenever she emptied it.

After several minutes of mutual musings, Alesa spoke. "Ellie, I was just thinking. Both of us could use a different kind of new start since neither of us likes the ones we already have. What do you say we plant a little garden just for the two of us."

"Could we really?" Ellie squealed. "I've never had my very own garden."

"Then it's settled." Alesa took off her garden glove and tousled Ellie's hair fondly. "Now we just have to decide what to plant. What's your favorite color?"

"Red!"

"Red . . . let me think . . . I have the perfect idea." Alesa smiled at the wide-eyed little girl. "We'll plant red radishes. They grow fast, and they're fun to eat. How would that be?"

"That would be the best! I can't wait to tell my daddy." She turned to leave, then turned back tentatively. "So I'll see you tomorrow after school?"

"I'll be looking for you."

That evening Alesa walked to Ellie's house and introduced herself to Ellie's father. "I'm Alesa Woodham," she explained to the uncertain man who opened the door. "I met your daughter today."

"Oh, so you're the garden lady," he said, visibly relaxing and smiling. "I'm David Spencer, Ellie's dad." He extended his hand in greeting. "She hasn't quit talking about you since she came home. I hope she wasn't too much trouble."

"She was delightful," Alesa reassured him. "Did Ellie tell you about our plan for a little garden?"

"Over and over and over again. She kept talking about planting her favorite color. She couldn't remember the plant's name, but she remembered that it was red."

"Yes, we're going to plant radishes. Would you mind if she came in for a snack after school?"

A Mother's Joy

"Sure. Ellie would love that. Her older brother gets home from school a few minutes before she does, so he'll be here until I get home."

Later Alesa baked chocolate-chip cookies as she jabbered away to her husband, telling him all about her new friend. She spent the next morning preparing the perfect spot for their new garden. She dug up the ground and added some fertilizer, then she raked the soil into a nice, loose surface.

When she heard the groan of the school-bus brakes in the afternoon, she was surprised at her own excitement. She went to the front porch and watched in anticipation as the bus door flew open. It seemed forever before her young friend descended the stairs. When Ellie saw Alesa, the little girl flashed a big smile and waved. "I have to tell my brother I'm home, then I'll be right over."

Minutes later Ellie bounded up the steps to Alesa's welcome: "Do you want to come in for a snack before we get to work? I made chocolate-chip cookies."

"Really?" Ellie asked wide-eyed. "I *love* chocolate-chip cookies."

"Me too," Alesa said. "They're my favorite."

A New Start

After sharing some cookies and milk, the gardeners went to the garage to gather their tools and seeds. "Here, Ellie. Let's put our things in this old wagon, then you can hop in and I'll pull you to our garden spot."

"Really?" Ellie asked again. "I've never ridden in a wagon before."

"This wagon has been in our family a long time. When my boys were little, I found it at a garage sale."

"What's a garage sale?"

"It's where people gather up all the stuff they don't need anymore and sell it from their garage or front yard to anyone who needs or wants it.

"Anyway, I bought this old wagon there and brought it home. I'd planned to just use it for garden work, but the boys loved it, so I sanded it down and painted it bright red. This second-hand wagon has given many rides in its life."

"What's *second hand?*" Ellie asked, her face screwed up in a quizzical expression.

"It means someone else had it before you did. Did anyone ever give you a dress after they got too big for it?"

"Uh-huh." Ellie nodded.

"Well, the girl who gave it to you was the 'first hand' to

have it. After she got too big for it, she passed it on to you. You were the 'second hand' to have it. Does that make sense?"

"Perfect sense!" Ellie exclaimed, satisfied. "So does that mean the wagon is 'third hand' for me?"

Alesa laughed. "I guess it does."

For the next hour, Ellie and Alesa dug little holes in the dirt and placed the tiny radish seeds inside. They covered the seeds, patted the dirt, and watered them with just the right amount of water. "That's all we can do for today," Alesa said as she gathered the tools. "If we water the ground every day after school and pull out any weeds that grow, we should have some baby radish plants in just a few days. Let's go inside and get something to drink before you go home."

Sitting at the kitchen table, enjoying ice-cold lemonade, Alesa asked Ellie about her day at school, and Ellie chatted comfortably with her new friend. It was nice having a child at her table again.

"What are you, Miss Lesa?" Ellie asked.

"What do you mean?"

"Are you a teacher or a doctor or an accountant, like my dad? You know, what are you?"

A New Start

"Well, for many years, I was a mom. But now that my boys are grown, I really don't know what I am."

Ellie wrinkled her brow and sat silently for a moment. Then her face lit up excitedly. "I know what you are, Miss Lesa."

"What am I, dear?"

"You're a second-hand mom!"

Alesa couldn't help but chuckle. "A second-hand mom?"

"Your kids had you for a mom until they grew up and got too big," Ellie reasoned out loud. "Now you're passed on to me. I get to eat your cookies and help you plant special gardens. You can be my second-hand mom, and I can be your second-hand kid!"

Alesa's heart felt as if it were about to burst with joy. "What a nice idea, Ellie." She reached across the table and squeezed her hand. "I've never had a little girl. I'd love to have you for a second-hand kid. And there's nothing I'd like better than to be your second-hand mom."

Maybe this new start wouldn't be so bad after all.

Mother is the one we count on
for the things
that matter most of all.

Katherine Butler
Hathaway